CAPE TOWN

Few of the world's landmarks are so instantly recognizable, or so intimately associated with a particular city, as Table Mountain. It towers more than 1 000 metres (3 300 feet) above the graceful thoroughfares of Cape Town, its two-mile long, almost dead-flat crest often wreathed in great, billowing tumbles of cloud known as the 'tablecloth'. On a clear day, though, those who reach the summit enjoy superlative views – of the metropolis below, its harbour and bustling waterfront, of the blue-grey Hottentot Hollands hills to the north, Robben Island and the Atlantic seaboard (*opposite, top*) to the west, the broad sweep of False Bay to the east and, far to the south, the rugged promontory of Cape Point. Most visitors make the ascent by cable-car (*above*), a safe, five-minute trip. At the top there's a restaurant, a souvenir shop from which you can send faxes (and letters bearing the Table Mountain postmark), observation sites (*opposite, top and bottom*), an orientation display (*opposite, centre*) and informative wall plaques describing the mountain reserve, its walking routes and its uniquely varied 'fynbos' flora. Among the reserve's wildlife is the rock hyrax, or 'dassie' (*right*).

Perhaps the most pleasant of Cape Town's piazzas is Greenmarket Square (*opposite, foreground*), a delightfully shade-dappled, cobbled area usually filled to its limits by street-traders' stalls crammed with craftwork and bric-a-brac, leather-ware, trendy clothing, costume jewellery and junk (among which you'll find the odd genuine antique). The square is girded around by some handsome and historic buildings, among them the Metropolitan Methodist church, built in Gothic-revival style in the 1870s, and the Old Town House (seen in the centre of the picture), which made its appearance more than a century earlier. The latter originally housed the Burgher Senate, or civic council, and the Burgher Watch, a combination of police force and fire brigade. It now embraces an art gallery whose pride is its collection of nearly 100 old Dutch and Flemish masterpieces.

Among Cape Town's livelier traditions is the Coon Carnival (*above*), held on the second day of each New Year, when an animated multitude of festive, brightly costumed minstrel troupes parade through the city's streets.

Prominent among Cape Town's landmarks are the stately Houses of Parliament (*left*), which face onto the city's lovely public gardens. Earlier administrations, both Dutch and British, were accommodated in the Castle (*below*), a five-sided, massive-walled fortress dating from 1678 and designed to guard the fledgling colony from invasion by sea. On view in the Castle are the former Governor's residence with its elegant furnishings and fine William Fehr collection of paintings, a military museum, a period house, the historic Dolphin Pool and, in the old Granary, an intriguing variety of artefacts unearthed during recent restoration work. At noon each day visitors may witness the changing of the guard.

Cape Town is home to a substantial Muslim community, many of whose members are descended from slaves brought from the East by the early colonists. It is a remarkably integrated society, bound together by culture and faith, its heritage most evident in the inner suburb of Bo-Kaap (also known as the Malay Quarter), a dense cluster of charming, flat-roofed little 18th-century houses nestling on the slopes of Signal Hill. Here, too, you'll find one of the Peninsula's six kramats (*opposite*) – shrines honouring Muslim spiritual leaders – that, together, form a 'holy circle'.

Cape Town, for long known as the 'Tavern of the Seas', owed its prestige and prosperity over the centuries to its strategic position on the sea route between Europe and the East – and to its harbour, set on the shore of Table Bay. Today the quaysides are quieter than they were in the halcyon days of sail and passenger steamer, but the port, South Africa's second largest after Durban, still welcomes maritime traffic – tankers and tramps, container vessels and glamorous cruise liners – from the world's seafaring nations. Parts of it are given over to the local fishing fleet (*opposite, top*) and to the craft of the Royal Cape Yacht Club (*opposite, centre and below*). More notable perhaps are the harbour's older sections, the Victoria and Alfred basins, formally inaugurated by England's Prince Alfred in 1860 and recently transformed into one of the city's premier leisure areas and tourist venues (*above*).

The Victoria and Alfred Waterfront is a strikingly imaginative scheme inspired by successful harbour redevelopment projects in Boston, Vancouver, Sydney and elsewhere, and it has brought new life and a refreshing vibrancy to Cape Town's dockland.

Much of the waterfront's charm is that it remains a working harbour, bustling with activity day and night. It is used by work-worn tugs, tenders and fishing boats; its dry-dock, built for the tall ships of long ago, still renders sterling service; fashionable offices, hotels and apartments have been built and more are planned.

But in essence the place is for the leisure-bent visitor, an extravaganza of sound and light, pubs and bistros, theatres, cinemas, museums, speciality stores, craft and produce markets, entertainment centres, playgrounds, promenades, public squares, marinas, a wine centre, a brewery, a helipad (for breathtaking round-the-Peninsula scenic trips) and steam-railway station. The main shopping mall is the cleverly converted and extended warehouse known as the Victoria Wharf (*opposite top, and right*).

Among the special attractions are the giant Imax cinema (whose screen is five storeys high; the sound-and-image system creates an experience approaching 'virtual reality'); the Two Oceans Aquarium, offering both above- and below-water insights into the region's kaleidoscopic marine life; and the South African Maritime Museum, which embraces floating exhibits as well as a wide variety of fascinating displays on terra firma.

Cape Town's 'Riviera' extends along some five kilometres of the Peninsula's western Atlantic seaboard, from Green Point south to Camps Bay – an affluent and densely developed coastal strip noted for its generally luxurious villas and apartment complexes, its rocky embayments, secluded coves and beautiful stretches of sand. The spectacular mountain backdrop is known as the Twelve Apostles, a series of grand, often cloud-wreathed sandstone and granite massifs (17 of them, despite their collective name) that form part of the Table Mountain range, and which flank the coastline as far as Hout Bay, 18 kilometres from the city centre.

The most fashionable of the seaside venues along the 'Riviera' is Clifton (*above and left*), hugging the slopes of Lion's Head in a spectacular setting of hillside and ocean and boasting four splendid beaches, each divided from its neighbours by ramparts of tumbled boulders. More spacious is the beach at nearby Camps Bay (*above right*), which is graced by broad sands, palm-fringed pavements, a tidal pool, shops, restaurants, a superlative colonial-style hotel – and which still manages to remain relatively unspoilt.

The sea along this stretch is azure blue, usually calm, and for most of the year too cold for comfortable bathing, though hardy surfers (*opposite, far left*) don wetsuits to brave the chilly rollers. But the area is sheltered from the summer south-easter, and it is a magnet for sunworshippers. By contrast the eastern, or False Bay, waters are warm but wind-swept.

The Atlantic coastal road winds its dramatically scenic way southwards to Hout Bay (*above*), a charming seaside residential town embraced by forested hills. The harbour serves as headquarters of the Peninsula's crayfish or rock-lobster fleet (*right*) though the sturdy, work-worn little boats harvest many other fruits of the sea, most notably great quantities of a shoaling, predatory fish known locally as snoek. Catches are sold from the quayside, which is also the venue for the annual and very popular Snoek Festival. Here, too, you'll find Mariner's Wharf, a lively and attractive emporium modelled on its San Francisco namesake.

From Hout Bay the marine drive twists up and over Chapman's Peak (*opposite, top*), a scenically breathtaking route slicing through cliffs that plunge, precipitously, to the blue ocean almost 600 metres below. Stunning vistas unfold along the road, which then descends into Noordhoek, famed for the wide white sands of its Long Beach (*opposite, below*).

cliffs (*right*), one can take in the vastness of the sky and the ocean; gulls and gannets and the occasional albatross wheel and swoop overhead; dolphins, seals, whales (*left*) and schools of tunny often sport in the waters far below. Visitors either walk the steep route to the top or take the shuttle-bus.

Cape Point is part of the extensive Cape of Good Hope Nature Reserve, noted more for its stunning scenery and floral wealth (about 1 200 'fynbos' species have been identified) than for its wildlife. But it does sustain a number of animals, among them the once-endangered bontebok and Cape mountain zebra, and four troops of chacma baboons (*right*). These last are thought to be unique within the primate world in their feeding habits: they subsist in part on marine foods, which they garner from the shoreline at low tide. Diaz beach (*top right*), one of the more popular spots within the reserve, is reached via a footpath.

It is off Cape Point that the *Flying Dutchman*, the ghost-ship with its fallen spars and tattered sheets, has occasionally been sighted (or so it is claimed) on its never-ending voyage. The legend was born in the 17th century, when Dutch sea-captain Hendrik van der Decken, his gale-battered vessel foundering, vowed to round the Cape of Good Hope even if it took him until Doomsday to do so.

Something of the same elemental mystery surrounds the massive headland at the tip of the Peninsula. From the most splendid of viewsites situated at the base of the old lighthouse high on the

'White as the sands of Muizenberg', wrote Rudyard Kipling, 'spun before the gale.' And the sands of this east-coast resort are indeed white and windblown, stretching in a graceful five-kilometre curve along the Peninsula's False Bay seaboard. Between Muizenberg (*above*) and next-door, more affluent St James, a quiet and rather old-fashioned village noted for its colourful beach-huts (*opposite, top*), is the thatched cottage to which the 19th-century tycoon and eccentric visionary Cecil Rhodes retired and in which, in 1902, he died. To the south beyond St James, are the substantial coastal towns of Fish Hoek with its pleasant expanses of beach (*opposite below left, and right*) and the historic naval centre of Simon's Town. Nearby Boulders, an attractive strip of seaside rock-and-sand, has been settled by a colony of threatened jackass penguins (*left*).

Among the earliest and arguably most splendid of the Western Cape's historic mansions is Groot Constantia, designed and built by the respected Dutch colonial governor Simon van der Stel at the end of the 17th century. It graces the green and pleasant Constantia Valley in the central Peninsula, a single-storeyed, thatched and handsomely gabled Cape Dutch homestead that was destroyed by fire in 1925 and then meticulously restored to the character and condition of its best years.

Van der Stel lived at Groot Constantia in his retirement, until his death in 1712, and it's said that his ghost can sometimes be seen strolling the avenue of stately oaks that bisects the grounds. Later, in 1778, the estate was taken over by Hendrik Cloete, who developed the vineyards to produce some of the world's finest wines, full-bodied vintages that found favour with the aristocracy of Europe (King Louis Philippe actually dispatched an emissary to the Cape to purchase a consignment). Hendrik Cloete also added a magnificent cellar, the work of the celebrated French architect Louis Thibault and noted for its superb, cherub-adorned pediment.

The estate still produces excellent wines, which visitors sample and buy *in situ*. There is also a museum that tells the story of wine-making through the centuries, and two inviting restaurants, including the Jonkershuis (*above*). Inside the Groot Constantia homestead (*opposite, top left*) you'll find an array of treasures –

elegant period furniture, exquisite porcelain from Holland, the Rhineland and East Asia; tapestries; paintings and *objets d'art*.

Groot Constantia is one of three historic and still-functioning wine estates within the valley which, together, form the Peninsula's only 'wine route'. The two other homesteads – Klein Constantia and Buitenverwachting – are more modest in scale and scope but, in their own way, just as attractive. A fourth, Alphen, now serves as one of the Peninsula's most atmospheric hotels.

On and below the slopes of Table Mountain are the southern sub-urbs, among the oldest of the city's residential areas (colonial farmers settled Rondebosch in the 1650s) and each boasting its distinctive features. Pride of Newlands is the Kirstenbosch Botanical Garden (*above*), a generous expanse of lush hillside terrain that sustains about half the country's 18 000 species of indigenous plants – proteas and ericas, mesembryanthemums (known locally as 'vygies'), ferns and cycads, colourful pelargoniums (from which the geranium has been hybridized), the red disa or 'Pride of Table Mountain' (*right*) and a great many others. Pathways lead through and beyond the cultivated areas; guided walks are laid on; visitor amenities include a gift shop and plant nursery and a pleasant restaurant.

Closer to the city are the broad acres of Rhodes' estate, embracing the university; the famed Groote Schuur hospital, scene of the world's first heart transplants; the state president's official residence, known for centuries as Groot Schuur ('Great Barn') and recently renamed Genadendal; Mostert's Mill (*opposite, below left*), which dates to the 1790s; and the Rhodes' Memorial complex (*above right*). This last, set high on the flank of Devil's Peak, is a Grecian-style 'temple' incorporating George Watts' powerful statue entitled 'Physical Energy' (*right*) and a large bust of the imperialist politician Cecil John Rhodes, beneath which is inscribed part of Kipling's moving tribute to 'the immense and brooding spirit'.

Cape Town is one of the southern hemisphere's leading tourist destinations, a major port of call on the international air and luxury sea-cruise routes. Here, the *Europa* lights up Table Bay (*above*), one of many sleekly graceful liners that have included the port on their itineraries. The city (*right*) and its surrounds have much to offer the visitor: good hotels, a myriad eating and drinking places, lively nightspots, the delights of the Waterfront, an inviting calendar of arts and sports, splendid beaches, the beauty of the Cape Peninsula and the not too distant winelands – and, of course, Table Mountain. These and other assets, both natural and man-made, place Cape Town in the forefront of the race to host the 2004 Olympic Games. If the bid is successful, this will be the first African city to stage the world's premier sporting extravaganza.